Pebble® Plus

T0004842

Our Fire Station

PEBBLE
a capstone imprint

by Mary Meinking

Pebble Plus is published by Pebble, an imprint of Capstone.
1710 Roe Crest Drive, North Mankato, Minnesota 56003
www.capstonepub.com

Library of Congress Cataloging-in-Publication data is available on the Library of Congress website.
ISBN 978-1-9771-1452-5 (library binding)
ISBN 978-1-9771-1784-7 (paperback)
ISBN 978-1-9771-1453-2 (eBook PDF)

Summary: A fire station helps keep our community safe. Community helpers work hard to keep a fire station running smoothly. Readers will learn about who works at a fire station, what the workers do, and what makes a fire station special. Simple, at-level text and vibrant photos help readers learn all about fire stations in the community.

Editorial Credits
Editor: Mari Schuh; Designers: Kay Fraser and Ashlee Suker; Media Researcher: Eric Gohl;
Production Specialist: Katy LaVigne

Photo Credits
Alamy: Phil Wills, 5; iStockphoto: BluIz60, 9, kali9, cover, LPETTET, 1, 13, martin-dm, 11; Getty Images: EyeEm/Marc Borchert, 15, Hero Images, 17; Newscom: Ingram Publishing, 7; Shutterstock: Alexxndr, 2 (notebooks), andreitlp, 19, Betelgejze, 3, Chantal de Bruijne, 2 (equipment), Mark Agnor, 24, mat277, back cover, 4, 6, 8, 10, 12, 14, 16, 18, 20, 22, Sundry Photography, 23, wavebreakmedia, 21

Note to Parents and Teachers

The Places in Our Community set supports national social studies standards related to people, places, and environments. This book describes and illustrates a fire station and the people who work there. The images support early readers in understanding the text. The repetition of words and phrases helps early readers learn new words. This book also introduces early readers to subject-specific vocabulary words, which are defined in the Glossary section. Early readers may need assistance to read some words and to use the Table of Contents, Glossary, Read More, Internet Sites, Critical Thinking Questions, and Index sections of the book.

All internet sites appearing in back matter were available and accurate when this book was sent to press.

Printed in the United States   5692

Table of Contents

Let's Visit a Fire Station!

Look at that big fire truck!
A fire truck is kept inside a
fire station. You will also find
tools and gear in a fire station.
Let's go to a fire station!

4

5

Who Works at a Fire Station?

Firefighters work at

a fire station. Some of them

work, eat, and sleep at

the fire station. They are

at the station day and night.

Other firefighters are
volunteers. They do not live
at the fire station. They have
regular jobs. They go to
the fire station when needed.

The fire chief is the boss.
He makes sure everyone does
their jobs. He trains firefighters
to put out fires. He wants them
to be safe while helping others.

What Firefighters Do

Some firefighters drive
fire trucks. Others climb
ladders. They spray water
from hoses to put out fires.
They work quickly to save lives.

After a fire, firefighters go back

to the station. They get ready

for the next call. They wash

the fire trucks inside the station.

They clean their gear.

Firefighters train at the station.
They practice what to do during
an emergency. They lift weights
in the exercise room. They need
to be strong to lift heavy hoses.

21
41

21
141

21
148

21
145

21
6

Firefighters are ready for anything. They help at fires and car accidents. They help people who are sick or hurt. Firefighters care about others.

Fire Stations are Busy Places

People visit the fire station.

Firefighters teach them

how to prevent fires.

Firefighters work hard to keep

everyone in the community safe.

20

Glossary

accident—an event that causes injury

emergency—an unexpected dangerous situation

firefighter—a person who is trained to put out fires

gear—supplies, tools, or clothes needed for a special purpose

hose—a long rubber tube that water flows through

prevent—to stop something from happening

volunteer—a person who chooses to do work without pay

Read More

Clark, Rosalyn. *A Visit to the Fire Station.* Minneapolis: Lerner Publications, 2018.

Hoena, Blake A. *A Visit to the Fire Station.* Mankato, MN: Capstone Press, 2018.

Kelley, K. C. *Fire Station.* Mankato, MN: Amicus, 2018.

Internet Sites

National Fire Protection Association: Sparky's Fire House
http://www.sparky.org/

Fire Safe Kids
http://www.firesafekids.org/games.html

U.S. Fire Administration
https://www.usfa.fema.gov/downloads/pdf/publications/fa_327_print.pdf

Critical Thinking Questions

1. List two things firefighters do at a fire station.

2. Name two pieces of gear that firefighters use.

3. What do firefighters do when they are not fighting fires?

Index